RAILROADS

Title page: Denver & Rio Grande Western narrow-gauge 2-8-2 480 is shrouded in steam during early morning servicing.
Preceding pages: A Norfolk & Western class 2-6-6-4 1218, traditionally a freight-hauler, roars through the heart of West Virginia coal country with an excursion train. *This page:* Just east of Laramie, this Denver to Laramie and return Union Pacific passenger special is caught in a snowstorm.

The Virginia & Truckee was a Nevada short line running south from Reno. Abandoned in the 1950's, it has been partially rebuilt as a tourist operation.

Laying down a heavy swathe of black smoke, Reading T-1 4-8-4 2100 is in charge of an excursion. *Opposite:* Charging through Old Fort, North Carolina, Norfolk & Western 2-6-6-4 1218 works a passenger excursion train. As such excursions draw the public, the 1218 sees plenty of work. *Overleaf:* Steam locomotives, such as former Great Western 2-10-0 Decapod 90 (a 1924 Baldwin Locomotive Works product), must have maintenance. Each morning the engineers of the Strasburg Rail Road in Pennsylvania lubricate and fine-tune the engines they are going to use that day.

RAILROADS

David C. Lustig

PORTLAND HOUSE

NEW YORK

This 1990 edition published by Portland House,
a division of dilithium Press, Ltd.
distributed by Crown Publishers, Inc.
225 Park Avenue South, New York, New York 10003

ISBN 0-517-68849-2
hgfedcba

Printed and bound in Spain

For rights information about the photographs in
this book please contact:

The Image Bank
111 Fifth Avenue, New York, NY 10003

To Grace, Jenny, and Pam.

Author: David C. Lustig

Producer: Solomon M. Skolnick
Designer: Ann-Louise Lipman
Editor: Terri L. Hardin
Production: Valerie Zars
Senior Picture Researcher: Edward Douglas
Editorial Assistant: Carol Raguso
Project Picture Researcher: Robert V. Hale

I N T R O D U C T I O N

Breathes there a child that is not fascinated by trains? Or for that matter, an adult? We rarely watch trucks or buses, but when we sit at a railroad crossing and wait for a train, invariably we look up and watch the procession.

First comes the locomotive, both powerful and smokey, and then the string of cars. If it is a passenger train, it will be filled with brief glimpses of people, sitting, reading, talking, and laughing. If it is a freight train, there's a good chance you will read the names of the railroads printed boldly or ever so demurely on the side of the cars. Large multi-state railroads such as Southern Pacific, Conrail, Burlington Northern, Norfolk Southern, CSX, and Santa Fe are mingled freely with the smallest of shortlines, the likes of which are Ventura County, Hartcomb & Slocomb, and Florida West Coast.

Often, our minds roam to where those freight cars have been, what cargoes they hold in their bellies and where they are going. Kitchen appliances, coal, airplane parts, food, lumber, newsprint, iron ore, crude oil, and people, to name but a few items, move in a non-stop, synchronized ballet of revving diesel locomotives, blinking and ringing crossing signals, and oscillating headlights piercing the inky night—a cacophony of noise. Then, as soon as the parade has past . . . silence. Bells stop, crossing gates return to attention and, when it is our turn to cross the now-burnished rails, a quick look down the tracks will reveal only an ever-shrinking image hustling to Seattle or Atlanta, Detroit or Los Angeles, New York City or St. Louis.

More than any other kind of landborne transportation before or since, trains have a continuing attraction. But they have not always been a strong and economical form of transportation. In the early 1800's, when the United States was young and not too steady on its feet, so too was railroading, a fledgling idea that no one at the time thought could revolutionize travel within just a few short decades.

The concept of traveling on a fixed bed of rails had been proven over and over since the late 1700's, first using mules for propulsion and then later, in the 1820's, a steam boiler on wheels. The steam-driven pistons were connected off-center to the wheels by rods, which in turn moved the rods that propelled the wheels.

The idea was sound, so sound that many people—canal owners, stagecoach owners, and freight companies—opposed the concept of building a railroad.

The first railroad built specifically to carry commercial freight (and any passenger who had the fare) was the Baltimore & Ohio, with service beginning in 1830. But the honor of the first steam engine to pull cars on a railroad goes to the South Carolina Canal and Railroad Company using the *Best Friend of Charleston* in December of that year.

From this beginning, there was no stopping railroading and, in 1831, the Camden & Amboy—now part of Conrail—put a steam locomotive named the *John Bull* (preserved in the Smithsonian) into service. To this engine and her sisters that ran on the original Camden, New Jersey to South Amboy (just south of Staten Island) railroad goes the honor of being fitted with the first cowcatchers. Meanwhile, rail lines began radiating out of Boston, Massachusetts and Providence, Rhode Island.

The Age of the Railroad Begins

As standardization of equipment began replacing experimentation, long-distance railroad routes were planned and constructed, including the New York & Erie Railroad from New York to Chicago, and the Pennsylvania Railroad operating between Pittsburgh and Philadelphia. By 1838, approximately 2,900 miles of railroad track were in operation.

By the middle of the nineteenth century, railroad fever was sweeping the nation and groups of investors were forming cartels and corporations specifically to build and operate this new form of transportation.

Chicago, with its central location, became a new railroad hub, with lines extending like an octopus in all directions. Other companies built from St. Louis and a fledgling railroad, the Rock Island, was one of the first to begin laying track westward from the Mississippi River.

Then came the American Civil War; just as man has used every other technological advance in wartime, so too were the railroads drafted.

It was the North that most effectively used its railroads in wartime, moving massive amounts of troops, supplies and munitions from rear areas to the front lines in days rather than weeks, its effective transportation web more easily adapting from carrying flour and wheat in peacetime. The South, due to the lack of standardization, was hampered by a comparatively disorganized rail system that did not allow free intermingling of equipment.

And since railroads were of strategic importance, the Civil War marked the first time in history that they became a military target, with their destruction considered a high priority to both sides. Raids by both Union and Confederate troops to destroy the enemy's locomotives, rolling stock, and track were common. The most famous raid, later immortalized by a number of motion pictures, was launched on April 12, 1862. Twenty Union soldiers planned to seize a train on the Western & Atlantic Railroad in Georgia and run it north toward Union lines, destroying everything connected to the railroad—tracks, bridges, communications, and rolling stock—behind it.

Dressed in civilian clothes and acting as typical Southerners, the men caught a train running between Atlanta, Georgia and Chattanooga, Tennessee. When the crew made a stop to let passengers eat lunch, the soldiers boarded the locomotive and, while a startled train crew watched from the dining room, released the brakes to begin their run northward.

For the next eight hours, the Union soldiers on board the locomotive named *The General* raced northward—with Southern soldiers and the conductor of the train they had stolen hot on their heels. All attempts to destroy bridges and communications lines failed, however, as the pursuers never allowed the Union men to stop long enough to complete any sabotage. Attempts by the raiding party to destroy the railroad by leaving burning boxcars in the middle of railroad bridges also failed, the pursuing Southerners arriving only moments later to push them off the bridges, derail them and continue their pursuit.

Finally, just south of the Tennessee state line, out of fuel and water and totally failing in their mission (except to perhaps cause a little chaos), the men disembarked from what was left of the train, heading into the woods to fend for themselves. Eventually all were captured. Some were later hung as spies—remember, they were all dressed in civilian clothes—and the rest sent to prisoner-of-war camps. Interestingly, *The General* and one of the locomotives the Confederates used to chase her, *The Texas*, are still in existence today and displayed at Chattanooga and Atlanta, respectively.

If this story seems vaguely familiar, perhaps you remember what is considered one of the finest silent movies ever made, *The General*, with Buster Keaton, or saw Walt Disney's 1954 movie, *The Great Locomotive Chase*, with Fess Parker (who later became better known to the television generation as Davy Crockett and Daniel Boone).

After the cessation of Civil War hostilities, all eyes of the nation turned West to a project conceived in the darkest days of battle, the building of the first transcontinental railroad. The need for such a railroad had always been on the mind of Abraham Lincoln and, on July 1, 1862, he signed into law the Pacific Railroad Act, which chartered two railroads, the Central Pacific and Union Pacific, to complete the job.

Almost as soon as the ink was dry on the document, the Union Pacific began assembling its initial base camp at Omaha, Nebraska. Shortly afterward, it laid its initial track westward toward the Pacific Ocean. At the same time, from the west, the Central Pacific began laying tracks eastward from Sacramento, California. The ultimate intention was to meet "somewhere in the middle," but the route, horizontally through the middle of the American West, was a tortuous one.

For the Union Pacific there was the vast emptiness of the great plains, followed by the Rocky Mountains, as more than 10,000 laborers (mostly of Irish extraction) laid an average of three to four miles of rail a day. Track gangs followed surveyor's markings to lay down ballast. These were followed by other gangs bringing ties, followed by the steel gangs spiking rail. It was a never-ending job, as men worked from sunrise to sunset, seven days a week, through all climates, temperatures, and storms of nature.

Over on the West Coast, thousands of imported Chinese laborers did most of the physical labor for the Central Pacific. Their first confrontation was the rugged Sierra Nevada mountain range. The many tunnels that had to be excavated and bridges that had to be built took a heavy toll on human life. And no sooner were the mountains conquered than the workers were confronted by hundreds of miles of arid Nevada desert.

There are many stories about how the two railroads met, but the most-often heard is that when they saw each other, opposing track-laying crews from the Union Pacific and Central Pacific just kept on working past one another, since each railroad's share of government funding depended on how many miles of track it laid!

But as the two railroads were nearing their final miles, the government had already selected a proposed site for the official celebration: Promontory Point, Utah, just north of the Great Salt Lake. The historic event took place on May 10, 1869.

Called "the wedding of the rails," it was the beginning of a new saga in American railroad history. Unfortunately, it was the end for other, uniquely American endeavors, such as the Pony Express and many freight-hauling wagon companies;

and for the free roaming of Native American tribes.

But on that day, the country was in celebration, with civic leaders, journalists, railroaders, and local Mormons from nearby Salt Lake City all attending.

With telegraph wires hooked up to a spike hammer, a golden spike was tapped into place in a specially finished railroad tie, the connection made by the hammer and spike going out through a communications line from coast to coast.

The last spike in, two locomotives, Central Pacific's *Jupiter* and Union Pacific's *Number 119*, slowly inched closer and closer until their cowcatchers touched, and the scene was immortalized by photographers and journalists. Official accounts cite gentlemanly conduct by all parties during the event, but eyewitnesses reported an incredibly raucous celebration that lasted for days.

As a side note, just moments after the ceremony, the heavily protected golden spike was quickly pulled out and removed from the scene, as was the special tie, to be replaced by a standard steel spike and rough-hewn tie. The spike is currently held by Stanford University Museum in Palo Alto, California.

With the initial line completed, other financiers and investors eagerly eyed the West as a yet untapped source of potential fortune, and plans were quickly drawn up for other transcontinental rail lines.

The linking of the West brought up another problem for railroad builders—gauge, or the width between the rails. In the early days of railroading, there seemed to be as many different gauges as there were railroads, with rail widths ranging anywhere from three feet between centers to almost six feet. Finally, with a few exceptions, every railroad agreed to four-feet, eight-and-a-half inches between rail centers.

The exceptions were the numerous three-foot-gauge railroads that were usually built for specific purposes—to service the gold mines, coal mines, and other bulk industries—that had to traverse extremely tough terrain. The principal advantage was size; narrow-gauge trains were smaller, therefore less money, and time had to be spent surveying, blasting tunnels, and laying rail. These lines flourished in various parts of the country, but were predominant in the Rocky Mountains.

Some were narrow-gauge divisions of standard railroads, such as the Denver & Rio Grande Western, which operated a far-flung empire of slim rails that reached into gold and silver country, using dozens of locomotives and thousands of employees.

Other narrow-gauge railroads, such as the Florence & Cripple Creek, sported luxurious sleeping cars with brass beds. The Silverton Railroad, which during its heyday was transporting between 25,000 and 50,000 tons of ore a year from the mines, had a line filled with tight curves and loops.

In the East, notable narrow-gauge lines included the East Broad Top, a mining railroad in Pennsylvania; and in the West, the Carson & Colorado—which was later taken over by the Southern Pacific. The Carson & Colorado ran for 300 miles through mostly barren desert from just south of Reno, Nevada to Keeler, California near Lone Pine. Again, mining was the principal motivation for building the line and during its operating days it transported millions of dollars of ore.

Before being abandoned in 1960, the Southern Pacific purchased a diesel to replace its three steam locomotives, making it the only regular narrow-gauge railroad to be fully dieselized in the United States. The South's best example of a narrow-gauge would be the Eastern Tennessee & Western North Carolina, known locally as "The Tweetsie."

But the core operation was in Colorado. Other railroad operations in the area—including the Rio Grande Southern (RGS)—were virtually unknown outside of railroad circles. The RGS was crucial to the atomic bomb effort of World War II, for it was the initial mode of transportation in moving the uranium ore from Colorado mines to the processing facilities. The Colorado and Southern operated extensively in the state, as well.

The future, however, was in standard-gauge railroading. By the turn of the century, the Great Northern, Northern Pacific, Milwaukee Road, Southern Pacific, Santa Fe, and Union Pacific all had their own lines reaching from approximately somewhere along the Mississippi River to the Pacific Coast, either directly or in conjunction with other railroads such as the Rock Island, the Denver & Rio Grande Western, and the Missouri Pacific.

And there was no stopping railroad expansion elsewhere. Railroads like the Southern, Louisville & Nashville, Atlantic Coast Line, and Seaboard Airline criss-crossed the South. The Illinois Central kept its main line from Chicago to New Orleans well-oiled with trains, as did its competition, Gulf, Mobile & Ohio, and Chicago & Alton. The Pennsylvania Railroad, New York Central, and Erie fiercely fought for New York-to-Chicago revenue, along with several smaller lines that combined end to end to serve the two great cities.

From a humble beginning, the American railroad reached its zenith—in terms of mileage—during World War I, with more than a quarter-million miles of route in the 48 contiguous states. Today, it is just over 190,000 miles.

At first glance, this lends credence to the argument that railroads are passé and in a steady decline. But that just isn't so.

Changes, Better and Worse

As nations and economies evolve, so do the transportation systems that support them. Trains replaced stagecoaches and freight wagons because railroading was a more efficient—and profitable—way of moving goods and people.

Trains opened up rural America to the rest of the world. Farmers shipped their harvests outbound on them and received finished goods from the city back in on them. The mail came by train—so did milk and butter from the local creamery. People rode them when shopping in the next town, getting to their dancing lessons or the dentist.

In turn, the trains and crews of these local lines became part of the fabric of the community. Every town had a station, every station an agent and every agent was a knowledgeable friend who knew not only when the train was coming and when it was leaving, but what it was bringing. The doctor came in on the train, the young draftee going to war went out on it.

After World War II, with a steady improvement in airplanes and federally funded highway systems, much of that changed. When the railroads opened the West, they had allowed people to travel and ship goods from the Mississippi River to the Pacific Coast in six or seven days, versus the six or seven weeks by stagecoach. Yet, where railroads didn't go, stage lines still flourished. It is interesting to note that the last stagecoaches were replaced by buses, not trains. (Indeed, many stage companies took the hint early on, eventually evolving into local and regional bus companies.)

The same order of things continues today. The United States has an excellent, although at this point, aging, highway system, with trucks and buses more efficiently handling short-haul requirements far faster and more economically than railroads. An argument can even be made for long-distance runs.

But try and economically handle 10,000 tons of coal by truck—something that is routinely handled by a single freight train. Or consider the fact that a dozen railroad men can take a 100-car train filled with ship containers from point *A* to point *B*, when it would take at least one man per container by truck to do the same job. If a company has to ship goods from Los Angeles to Santa Barbara, New York to Baltimore, St. Louis to Kansas City, or any other short distance, trucks should and can win every time. But when it comes to bulk goods, such as iron ore, coal, or wheat or massive quantities of finished products such as automobiles, kitchen appliances, newsprint, and whatever else the American economy needs, nothing can beat a railroad.

Passengers are no exception.

Since the majority of long-distance passengers are traveling for the specific purpose of coming from one place and going to another, they have, of course, abandoned passenger trains for airplanes. If a salesperson needs to travel from Los Angeles to Chicago on business, would he prefer two days on a train or three hours on a jet? There's no comparison.

Yet there is still a viable place for railroad passenger trains.

On one hand, passenger trains, like buses, go many places that scheduled airlines do not. On the other hand, once out of the big cities and into the countryside, passenger trains provide one of the last great ways to see America the way our ancestors did: *sans* billboards, concrete highways, and neon-lit, look-alike, fast-food restaurants. It is the strength of long-distance passenger travel and one that Amtrak has successfully exploited in various "See America" campaigns.

By the 1900's, railroads reached practically every city, town, and hamlet in the country and one of the most envied jobs in the entire country was that of a locomotive engineer. Look, for example, how Casey Jones, after being killed when the train he was working slammed into the rear of another that had yet to clear the mainline, has been immortalized over the years. Nothing could beat the adoration of the young boys who would congregate down by the depot to watch *The Express* or any other train thunder by. Better yet were the local trains that stopped to drop off a few freight cars or pick up a few passengers. With the "steed" at rest, it was common to climb up into the cab and see what the engineer's office looked like, the myriad gauges and valves looking almost impossible to master.

This was the heyday of American passenger trains and, in particular, sleeping cars, of which the best-known were invented by George M. Pullman.

Most early sleeping cars were converted from existing day coaches. And rode like them. During the middle of the Civil War, Pullman unveiled a totally new design, a car he christened "Pioneer," with wider and taller dimensions than any other existing passenger car of the time. While it fascinated the public, it did nothing for the railroads since, due to its width, it was unable to fit next to many existing railroad station platforms.

But fate, however unkind to the rest of the country, was on the inventor's side, and when President Abraham Lincoln's body was returned to Illinois, from Chicago onward the family rode in Pullman's Pioneer. A short time later, Ulysses S. Grant, then President, rode the car. Events such as these, combined with new sleeping car inventions, eventually propelled Pullman to become the premier sleeping-car builder.

After the linking of the Central Pacific and Union Pacific at Promontory Point in 1869, Pullman enjoyed even more success. For those who could afford the extra fare, the journey from coast to coast could be enjoyed in the daytime and slumbered through peacefully in a comfortable bed at night.

This was also a period in American history when, if someone wanted speed, they looked toward the railroads. One such someone was Walter Scott, better known as Death Valley Scotty.

Scott was a miner, or so he said, who searched California's Death Valley for gold. On a whim, the story goes, he decided he wanted to be the fastest man between Los Angeles and Chicago.

With that thought, he walked into the passenger office of the Santa Fe in Los Angeles one afternoon and paid $5,500 for a special one-time, one-way train to beat all existing records. Having a flair for the theatrical, he dubbed it "The Coyote Special."

It was a public relations department's dream. Here was a man not connected to the railroad, plunking down hard-earned cash to ride a special train—the fastest train—from one end of the Santa Fe to the other. No expense had to be paid to get the word out, either, and when Scott's automobile pulled up by the station, a crowd of curious people waited to greet him.

At exactly 1:00 P.M. on Sunday, July 9, 1905, a locomotive, baggage car, dining car, and Pullman left Santa Fe's LaGrande Station for points east. On board were Scotty, his wife, various hangers-on and at least one journalist.

The Santa Fe made careful plans to ensure all went well on Scott's record-breaking ride. All along the route, 19 specially prepared engines were strategically stationed to make sure locomotive changes were done as quickly as possible. Attaining speeds of close to 100 miles per hour, fighting heavy grades through California's Cajon Pass, spanning a seemingly endless desert from Barstow, east over the Colorado River and through Williams, Gallup, and Albuquerque, the train flashed by, with well-wishers frequently gathering lineside to watch *The Coyote Special* pass. And every time the train crew met or exceeded the schedule, Scotty would reward them by passing out freshly minted silver dollars.

While it seemed to be the most exciting thing in the world to do from lineside, reports from inside the train were sometimes a little less dignified.

Scott stressed speed and speed he got. While breaking existing records across the flatlands was not particularly hard on train, body, or soul, making the best time ever through tortuous mountain passes and around tight curves was. While safety was utmost on every engineer's mind, not one of the 19 crews assigned to the run was going to take the blame if, for some reason, the 46-hour record were not broken.

The first indication that speed and refined passenger travel couldn't really co-exist occurred going through Cajon Pass in Southern California. From Los Angeles to San Bernardino, about 100 miles east, the line was flat and easy to travel; from San Bernardino, however, the tracks go north through the mountains to get to the desert community of Barstow before again turning east. Regularly scheduled Santa Fe passenger trains slowed down considerably through the winding canyons and on the steep grades in order to make the ride comfortable. But not on this run.

Santa Fe crews did their utmost to push, but not exceed, the safety limits through the mountains and inside the rear car. Even so, unsuspecting passengers were routinely doused with champagne or thrown off-balance as the train whipped through the mountains.

Once on the desert floor, things quieted down a little, only to start up again as *The Coyote Special* wended its way across the Rocky Mountains and, except for lightning-fast engine changes (with the new engines already waiting on the mainline for the train), the speed show never abated. Scott flashed through Dodge City and Emporia and Kansas City in a blur, reaching Chicago at 11:54 A.M. on July 11th, besting even Santa Fe's promise by making the 2,265-mile run in an incredible 44 hours and 54 minutes. *The Coyote Special* was history.

And what of Scott and party? After spending a few days in Chicago, he and his wife boarded a regularly scheduled Santa Fe passenger train home, just like other paying passengers.

Steam engines, no matter who owned them or what their size, were classified by the number of axles they had, and in what order. The system created by F.H. Whyte in the nineteenth century is relatively simple: if a locomotive has a small wheel in front by the pilot, and four larger spoked ones, then a small one under the cab, it is a 2-8-2 design. A similar locomotive without the small wheel under the cab would be a 2-8-0. A larger locomotive with two small wheels, four large ones and then two small ones would be a 4-8-4, and so on.

And each type had a name. For example, 2-8-2's were known as Mikados, because the design was first used in Japan; and 4-6-4's were Hudsons because the first railroad to use them was the New York Central, which paralleled the Hudson River.

But locomotive design doesn't indicate the speed, or lack of it, that a locomotive can attain. Rapidity was becoming a rarity on many railroads, and by the 1910's, "dragging"—tying every freight car in the train yard onto the locomotive and somehow getting over the road, no matter how slowly—was in vogue.

Monstrous new steam locomotives—in reality just extensions of existing designs—began emerging, their small drivers amply suited for tremendous tractive effort, enabling them to start very heavy trains.

Small drivers, however, meant a low top-end speed and 25 to 30 miles per hour became a speedy snail's pace for American railroads.

But quantity was not quality. With the coming of World War I, it became apparent that railroad management was suffering from serious omissions in efficient operation. In short, the government needed the railroads to provide dependable, on-time—and fast—transportation. The railroads, despite excellent equipment, couldn't do it.

The federal government decided to do what private enterprise could not and, in 1916, Congress authorized the United States Railroad Administration—USRA for short—to takeover and efficiently operate America's railroads during wartime.

In a move uncommon to typical government bureaucracy, the agency and its managers, many of whom had been solicited from the railroads the USRA was now controlling, sought to streamline and consolidate locomotive designs, terminal facilities, and operating conditions. Seven standardized steam locomotive designs, ranging from diminutive 0-6-0 switchers to 4-8-2 Mountains, were blueprinted and offered to railroads needing to acquire new motive power. So were freight cars and passenger cars, yard designs, and equipment repair all the way down to the types of tickets and forms to be used. After the cessation of hostilities, the various corporate structures of the railroads, kept intact during the USRA reign, were again allowed to take over their own destinies. (Long after World War I, many railroads ordered modified USRA steam-engine designs from locomotive builders.)

But it was the new steam-locomotive designs of the mid-1920's that brought railroading a quantum-leap forward and introduced a new phrase into the vocabulary: super power.

Lima, the smallest of the three major steam builders (the others were Baldwin near Philadelphia and American Locomotive near Albany), could sometimes be the most innovative. The Ohio builder unveiled a new type of freight locomotive, designed to competitively haul long freight trains. Thanks to larger drivers and new methods of efficiently using steam, it could do so at much faster speeds. Perhaps the best comparison would be the airlines jumping from propeller-driven airplanes to jet-powered. Suddenly, it was a whole new ball game.

The new engines also incorporated a new wheel designation of 2-8-4: a two-wheel front truck to guide the engine through switches, eight large drivers (four on each side of the locomotive) and a four-wheel trailing truck which helped support the large firebox. The engines were dubbed "Berkshires" because they were originally purchased by the Boston Albany for use in the Berkshire mountains. They were an instant success, and a number of railroads immediately began purchasing the new type of power. Heavy tonnage was still important, but now speed mattered as well.

In the next decade, the 2-8-4 design and its larger sister, the 2-10-4, were produced by all builders, and could be found in almost all areas of the nation save the Pacific Northwest. Many of these locomotives were among the last steam engines regularly used by American railroads in the late 1950's.

By 1929, however, most of the railroads, which had roared into the decade with the same gusto as the rest of the country, were in trouble. When the effects of the Great Depression fully hit the country at the start of the 1930's, most lines, like many other businesses, had filed for bankruptcy and were being run by court-appointed receivers.

The Electric Railroads and the Coming of the Diesel

Diesel locomotives are commonly thought of as a product of the 1940's and later. In reality, various forms of diesel engines, which owe their existence to their German creator, Dr. Rudolf Diesel, were experimented with as early as the turn of the century. Although some in railroad management were visionary enough to see practical applications of the diesel, for the most part, it was just a passing curiosity. Steam, everyone said, would always be king, even though other forms of propulsion, namely electrification, were already operating in a number of areas.

Even limited acceptance of the diesel would have to wait until the mid-1920's and the combining of brainpower of three giants: General Electric, the American Locomotive Company (a major steam locomotive manufacturer), and Ingersoll-Rand. The result was a 300-horsepower "box-cab" locomotive, so named because it looked like a rectangular box sitting on wheels with windows on the end and sides for the crew to look out from. It was a shaky start for the diesel invasion that would eventually revolutionize railroading. Meanwhile, large-scale electrification of American railroads could be found as early as just after the turn of the century when the New York, New Haven & Hartford converted its New York City to Stamford, Connecticut line from steam.

Indeed, most electric railroad operations began life as steam lines. The conversion to electrification was usually made because of safety—especially on lines where there were many tunnels and a buildup of steam engine smoke could asphyxiate the crews. The Pennsylvania Railroad was a big user of electric propulsion, stringing wire through much of the eastern half of its system. Examples of large main-line electrification projects out West could be found on the Great Northern as it plowed through the Cascades in the Pacific Northwest and the Milwaukee Road, with more than 650 miles of electrified lines. Today, the majority of electric operations are in the East, and predominantly on Amtrak.

But electrification proved to be a viable alternative to traditional steam locomotive power. When early diesels began to appear, most industry experts may have publicly chortled, but privately, they realized that steam might be getting a run for its money. That point was brought home when steam locomotive companies, including Baldwin (the largest), began to look at designing and building diesel locomotives. Not so much because they might be better than steam engines, said one mechanical engineer, but rather the locomotive builders were always interested in providing a "wide spectrum of propulsion to their customers." Which meant that everyone thought there might be something to diesel propulsion and nobody wanted to risk being left out in the cold.

By the 1930's almost everyone was investigating diesel propulsion, including General Electric, American Locomotive, Baldwin, Lima, and a relative newcomer to the fray, the Electro Motive Corporation of Chicago. This company had been purchased in 1930 by General Motors and renamed it Electro Motive Division (EMD). Today, this division is one of the giants of domestic diesel locomotive production.

The first mass-produced diesels were nothing if not ugly boxes, simply designed to be functional. They came, with a few exceptions, in two basic sizes: small units ranging from 300 to 1,000 horsepower, for use in switching yards, especially in smokeless areas like Manhattan, and larger 2,000-horsepower models designed to haul passenger trains. EMD and others designed lightweight articulated streamlined passenger trains around their new diesel power plants, ushering in style as well as speed. Shortly after, similarly styled passenger diesels, capable of pulling either streamlined equipment or traditional, railroad passenger cars, were introduced. They first appeared on the Baltimore and Ohio and the Atchison, Topeka & Santa Fe.

As the 1930's progressed, diesel locomotives became larger and more powerful and, most importantly, more reliable. Not a novelty anymore, they had many advantages over steam engines: they needed less attention, could work more hours with less servicing, were not as polluting, and were cheaper to maintain.

But the biggest attack on the steam bastion came in 1939, the year that General Motors Electro Motive Division brought out its then-revolutionary 1,350-horsepower FT locomotive. Semi-permanently coupled in pairs and, for demonstration purposes, put together in a set of four units, the FT was sent by its owner on a whirlwind barnstorming tour to almost every major railroad in the country as a goodwill ambassador.

And what an ambassador it was. On every railroad it visited it bested steam in either time from terminal to terminal, amount of fuel used, cost of maintenance, and/or percentage of availability. Most steam engines were able to go only a certain number of miles before they had to be pulled off and cleaned, lubricated, and serviced. But not the FT. Add fuel, watch the water, and make sure the lube oil is adequate, and let it go in any kind of weather.

When the tour was over, orders came flooding in, with the first production model going to the Santa Fe, which eventually stabled 320 of the machines. The Santa Fe had been very impressed by the FT's performance and was eager to try it out in the deserts of Texas, New Mexico, Arizona, and California. In many desert locations where the water was not suitable for steam locomotives, not only did the Santa Fe have to haul freight and passenger trains, it had to haul solid tank car trains of water into the bad areas. The FT would do away with all that; the only pure water needed on board was for the crew to drink.

As Baldwin and Alco looked for effective ways to counter EMD's FT, they brought out their own designs to show the railroads. But another player came into place to forever change the face of American railroading: World War II.

By 1939, the dark clouds of armed conflict were already gathering in Europe and the Orient. Most railroaders figured it was only a matter of time until the United States was actively involved.

The government thought so, too, and shipments of government goods and equipment in the United States began to increase as war material production, for both the Allies and the U.S., began to double, then triple, then quadruple. Literally overnight, many sleepy railroads were forced to wake up to the new amount of freight. Even many busy railroads became inundated. More motive power was needed.

As if everyone heard the same command, almost every major railroad turned to every major locomotive builder and said, "More!" Not just of steam engines, but diesels, switchers, electrics, road engines, passenger engines, freight haulers, anything. And the builders responded, working three shifts 24 hours a day, building new facilities and designing new products. But in 1942, the government again came into the railroad picture, this time not to take over the railroads but to control what the locomotive builders were putting out.

On the surface, it seemed to make sense to let the various builders construct whatever they wanted. After all, the railroads knew what they needed. But it was more complicated than that. Diesel power plants were needed for other things besides railroad locomotives—such as submarines and small surface vessels—and only government allocation could guarantee a steady flow to the most needy.

Under the jurisdiction of the War Production Board, American Locomotive and Baldwin, along with various smaller builders, were told they could construct whatever steam locomotives they wanted but, as far as new diesel construction, only yard switchers could be built. And EMD was told they could only build main-line freight locomotives. Passenger diesels, experiments, and research would all have to wait.

While some railroad historians believe that the government's decision to let EMD continue building road diesels (where the real profit in diesel-locomotive sales is) allowed the builder to take unfair advantage of its competition, it must be pointed out that there was plenty of work for everyone; more, in fact, than could have ever been handled even if there had been a fourth major diesel builder.

Diesel prime movers were needed everywhere, and companies like Baldwin expanded into Army tank production. Alco and Baldwin were able to make sizable profits on their switcher lines, which were already well established and proven to be dependable equipment. Still, it can be argued that EMD was given the advantage of no competition for a number of years as the company worked the bugs out of its road units, putting it in an excellent post–World War II position.

But this was just one squabble in an industry that needed every locomotive, regardless of whether it was steam or diesel.

Hundreds and thousands of locomotives sitting in rust piles and junk lines throughout the country during the Depression were overhauled and pressed back into service. Unnecessary rail travel by civilians was discouraged and anyone who could work was hired. Every yard seemed to be filled with loaded freight cars and dispatchers were kept busy 24 hours a day with five, 10, and sometimes 20 times the pre-war load of traffic. Somehow the fabric of railroading held together, transporting troops, tanks, war materials, guns, ammunition, and anything else needed by a modern army, on top of the existing freight and passenger traffic. Coastal tankers, which before the war freely paralleled the Atlantic and Pacific coasts, were forced into the harbors by the menace of enemy submarines; solid trains of oil-laden tank cars took their place, running up and down the coasts.

Defense plants sprung up where cows and horses had once grazed, needing rail lines to bring raw materials in and haul finished guns, tanks, and trucks out. Even the barest of down-on-its-luck short lines found profit in moving war traffic, with a new air base or army camp on-line meaning the transportation of hundreds of freight and passenger cars per week.

It was a great time to own stock in a railroad, but it was a blessing in disguise for the railroads when World War II finally ended. They were, in a word, tired.

Locomotives and freight cars that should have been retired a decade before had been kept running because there was nothing with which to replace them. Track crews never seemed to have ample time to shut down a section of rail to realign and ballast it, and replace loose tie plates and bolts properly. Everything was done catch-as-catch-can. Fortunately the war ended before such antics could catch up with the railroads.

Most railroads, their coffers brimming with World War II profits, were able to stay out of the receivership courts they were in a decade earlier, but some, now devoid of the extra income, quickly returned to the malaise of the '30's.

Many short lines and branch lines that had been on their last legs when World War II broke out and had become vital to the war effort, began going back to sleep. Service was cut back from daily to once a week or, even worse, abandoned outright. But for those healthy railroads that had not only survived but prospered, it was time to rebuild.

Ancient equipment was singled out and sent to the scrap heap as new freight and passenger cars were ordered in record numbers from builders. Everybody was re-equipping. Freight cars were all-steel designs now and companies such as Pullman-Standard—an outgrowth of the original Pullman sleeping car company—were introducing standardized lines of boxcars, flatcars, gondolas, and hoppers.

And passenger car orders went through the roof.

The streamlined-passenger-car era, which had begun in the 1930's on the Union Pacific's *City of San Francisco*, Illinois Central's *Green Diamond*, and the many Zephyr trains of the Chicago, Burlington & Quincy, had been quickly curtailed with the advent of World War II. Now it began again in earnest. The older, drab-green heavyweight cars became a thing of the past as glimmering stainless steel fluting enveloped everything from diesel locomotives to Pullmans, coaches, observation cars, and even baggage cars.

Railroads clamored to replace their old, heavyweight, passenger train equipment with new, lightweight, stainless-steel designs for their premier trains. Manufacturers like Budd and American Car & Foundry were the new recipients of the railroads' wealth as entire streamlined trains were ordered.

New train names mingled with old ones as the railroads offered passengers both luxury and speed. And train names, especially on each railroad's premier train, were designed to stimulate the imagination. The New York Central may have called it #25 or #26 in the timetable, but the advertising people called it *The 20th Century Limited*. The Pennsylvania Railroad had *The Broadway*, the Great Northern *The Empire Builder*, the Northern Pacific *The North Coast Limited*. There was *The Sunset* and *The Coast Daylight* on the Southern Pacific, *The Panama Limited* on the Illinois Central, Seaboard

Air Line's *Orange Blossom Special*, and perhaps the most famous train of them all, Santa Fe's *Super Chief*.

And there was something new to offer passengers: the dome car. Conceptualized by a diesel locomotive engineer, the dome car was first put in service by the Chicago, Burlington & Quincy. Originally designed with enough room for only about three dozen passengers to experience the high-level, 360-degree view, various modifications soon followed, including domes that were the full length of the passenger car and, on some railroads, a dome lounge car, affording partying passengers an unparalleled view of the world above and around them.

Railroads soon found themselves back on the front line when the government asked them to pick up the baton for freight movement during the Korean Conflict of the early 1950's. The railroads willingly obliged. This conflict was nowhere near the size or scope of World War II, and the railroads easily incorporated the extra trains into their schedules.

As the 1950's continued, railroads began losing more and more money on their passenger trains. For many, it was partially their fault for not having tried to cater to the ever-changing needs of the passengers; but mostly it was because two new players had entered the transportation scene: airplanes and interstate highways.

Domestic airlines, a novelty for the rich before World War II, came into their own, and passengers understandably took to them like ducks to water. Some railroads made a valiant effort to stay in the passenger business, vowing to run their trains to the best of their ability or not run them at all. Others tried to subtly sabotage their remaining passenger trains so the Interstate Commerce Commission (ICC), the regulatory body that controlled them, would allow those trains to be discontinued. For every railroad that made attempts to run clean, on-time passenger trains, there was another railroad equally committed to substandard equipment, dirty cars, and missed schedules.

But it was the interstate freeway system that drove the last nail into the coffin of most independent railroad passenger trains. With wide concrete highways cutting through previously impenetrable mountains and deserts, it was now possible, for example, to drive from Los Angeles to San Francisco in about eight hours. The train, on the other hand, took 11 or 12 hours, and when you got there you didn't have the convenience of your car.

The railroads tried to convince the ICC that, if only they could shed their money-losing, secondary passenger trains and concentrate on their first-class, main-line passengers, they could again be solvent transportation partners. Then, as the branch-line and secondary trains began to come off the timetable, it was clear this would not be the answer in shearing debt. The same argument was invoked again, with railroad lawyers telling the ICC that, if only they could get out of the passenger business, all would be well.

Time and again in the 1950's and 1960's, those who loved to ride passenger trains found themselves buying tickets for last runs. And in many cases, what was left really wasn't worth traveling on, anyway. Linoleum took the place of carpet in passenger cars on many routes, equipment was dirty, heaters didn't work in the winter, and air conditioners failed in the summer. More than one railroad removed dining cars altogether and replaced them with automat cars filled with brightly lit machines vending sandwiches, candy, and coffee, usually tasting like they had been prepared weeks before. To travel by train, said one wag, was similar to traveling steerage on the *Titanic*.

The Coming of Amtrak

If private industry were still in charge of trains today, then—except for a few high-density areas, such as Boston to Washington, D.C.—trains would be freight only. Railroad experts have determined that during the heyday of rail travel in the 1920's, there were slightly more than 21,000 regularly scheduled passenger trains. By the late 1960's, that number was down to about 425. On one hand, we can ridicule the railroads for not providing good service; on the other hand, if you were an accountant for a railroad and could see no way to end the flood of red ink, you too might recommend dumping passenger trains at almost any cost. Enter Amtrak.

Amtrak—American Track—is the short name for the National Railroad Passenger Corporation (NRPC), which was created by the federal government to help keep the passenger train alive. As it became obvious that the private railroads couldn't do it, the government decided to step in.

But not out of the goodness of Uncle Sam's heart.

In reality, there was—and is—a genuine need for passenger trains, capable of servicing cities and towns not well served by airlines or buses.

So, with government funds, Amtrak was inaugurated on May 1, 1971 to create a basic, railroad-passenger transportation system.

Selected passenger equipment, locomotives, and passenger stations were gladly sold by the railroads and, with three exceptions—the Chicago, Rock Island & Pacific; the Denver & Rio Grande Western, and the Southern—all rail travel, except commuter operations, was run solely by Amtrak.

Initial operations were a disaster. Operating over the now freight-only railroads, Amtrak owned no railroad right-of-way of its own. Equipment was often badly deteriorated, with passenger cars and locomotives averaging 15 to 25 years in age. Their condition had been made worse by deferred maintenance.

But Amtrak officials were not about to give up. Cars were cleaned, torn seats sewn, new interiors designed and installed, locomotives given overhauls and new paint jobs, and personnel were given lessons, all but lost on the railroads, on how to treat the customers. The reservation and billing system was brought literally into the Space Age by modeling it on airline systems. In less than 18 months, Amtrak, while still operating heavily in the red, managed to reverse the steady decline of railroad passengers.

Since its inception almost two decades ago, Amtrak has implemented new passenger cars, new locomotives, new stations, and a new attitude about train travel. In addition, the route structure has changed, with some money-losing routes curtailed and new routes added.

Amtrak has also not been afraid to look at what has worked in the past. One of the more innovative outings that rail-passenger service had taken was Santa Fe's *El Capitan*, which featured taller-than-normal cars, permitting an upper deck of seats and a lower deck of sleeping berths. Borrowing a page from the Santa Fe, most of Amtrak's long-distance trains now operate with these cars, affording passengers an unparalleled view.

Local runs haven't suffered either, with Amtrak introducing a line of intercity equipment that rivals most airlines, complete with comfortable seats, wide windows, public address system, and train heating and air conditioning that really works.

And while many Amtrak lines do not make money, there have been some surprising success stories.

The Coast Starlight, operating from Los Angeles to Seattle, is almost always booked solid and reservations for the summer months must be made weeks in advance. The Boston–New York–Washington, D.C. corridor is another money-making operation; and Amtrak has not only increased the number of trains and improved their on-time performance, it has physically purchased that vital section of railroad, putting the line under its tough guidelines for maintenance. Another profit-making run is the Los Angeles-to-San Diego *San Diegans*, down to a low of three a day each way when Amtrak took over. Now operating at eight a day each way, it includes a train that continues to Santa Barbara, some 90 miles north of Los Angeles.

And then there is Amtrak's special service to and from Florida, where passengers and their automobiles are hauled down in one train. The passengers enjoy a regular passenger car while the autos are lashed down inside enclosed freight cars.

Today, there are few pieces of original railroad-passenger equipment left in the fleet. What still remains is being phased out and replaced as rapidly as budgets allow.

As Amtrak navigates the current climate, always fending off federal budget cuts from the Congress which controls its purse-strings, it has proved that passenger train travel is a viable alternative to air and bus travel. No longer is train travel strictly a haven for the old, those afraid to fly, or those who travel to places where the other two don't go. If you're in a rush, say Amtrak officials, take a plane, but if you want to enjoy the scenery and have a good time, get into "Training."

Railroading Outside the United States

After World War II hostilities ended, most of other countries' railroads were in far worse physical shape than those of the United States. Because of the railroads' strategic military value, advancing armies assaulted them just enough to cripple but not enough to destroy, so they could be used by the victors. (In the Pacific, however, where Japanese railroad facilities were considered a key factor in crippling that country's ability to move men and equipment quickly, every effort was made to lay waste to Japanese transportation lines.)

In Europe, the railroads were a prime target for American and British precision bombing, with every freight car, marshalling yard, and major bridge and rail junction being rained on with bombs. And what aircraft couldn't do, underground

resistance fighters attempted, sabotaging troop trains and blowing up bridges wherever they could. And woe to the train caught out in the open by roving Allied fighters.

Conversely, retreating forces wanted to destroy as much as possible, to make it difficult for the enemy. Knowing this, the railroad battalions followed right behind American soldiers after the D-Day invasion at Normandy, June 6, 1944. Rostered with experienced railroaders from American companies, these men refurbished rail lines, brought with them their own locomotives and rolling stock, and re-established train operations in favor of the Allies in record time.

After World War II, due largely to the Marshall Plan (in which massive American aid was given to war-torn countries to rebuild themselves), all rail lines were rebuilt as quickly as possible. Economists had realized that most countries could not exist without a substantial rail network to move goods.

Today, the major national railroads are state-run (with the exception of Canada, where the privately owned Canadian Pacific competes with the government-controlled Canadian National). And because, as wards of the government, there is less of a demand to make them profit-making, the railroads are often seen as an excellent area to put the unemployed.

With not much incentive to make money, but instead to provide a basic service, there is less urgency to replace older locomotives and rolling stock with more efficient new designs. For the train fan, that has been a boon.

Big-time, main-line steam, which had died in the United States at the end of the 1950's, can still be found in limited amounts in South Africa, China, and the Soviet Union. China, for one, is still producing steam locomotives, and has just exported three medium-sized 2-8-0's to American tourist railroads.

Wherever steam locomotives are replaced, it has been with the diesel, which now for the most part competes with electric railroading—and is far more prevalent overseas, especially in Switzerland and the Soviet Union.

Foreign diesel designs have a little more variety than their American cousins, and world travelers can come across engines exported by Japan, Czechoslovakia, England, France, Germany, India, the Soviet Union, and China, besides those from the U.S. made by General Electric and General Motors.

Passenger trains are absolute necessities throughout the world. From Paris to New York City and Tokyo to Rio de Janeiro, complex commuter train networks are invaluable in keeping the human tide flowing.

But while government control can be a toe-hold to the past, in some countries, such as Japan, England, and France, it can be an entrée to the future.

Plagued by increasing populations and inadequate roadways, governments are constantly trying to exploit rail travel to become faster. Witness Japan's Bullet train, regularly operating at speeds in excess of 120 miles per hour. And newer French products are hitting 150.

Such speed can safely be obtained regularly by providing rail lines that have no road-crossings, a lack of slower freight traffic competing for space, and a sophisticated computer system backing up dispatchers.

For the rest of the world, high-speed passenger trains have only a limited value. Maintaining and upgrading traditional freight and passenger rail lines is the priority, and it shows no sign of slowing up, especially when it comes to tourism.

Many countries—especially England—abound in railroad museums that draw enthusiasts from every country. Inexpensive tourist rail passes are finding increasing acceptance throughout the world; this not only increases the ridership of intercity passenger trains with tourists, but also allows those same tourists to make sightseeing stops in towns and villages they might not otherwise be able to visit.

Railroading Today

Railroading today is as crucial to the American economy as it was in the 1860's. To keep up with the times, however, a railroad has to be flexible, cost-effective, and innovative; and looking for new ways to trim the fat and turn a profit.

Locomotives, by far the largest interest to most train watchers, have evolved over the years. Today, General Motors Electro Motive Division at LaGrange, Illinois and General Electric in Erie, Pennsylvania are the two primary builders, offering individual units that can reach 4,000 horsepower. They are fuel-efficient, use on-board computers to monitor systems and are capable of working for months without stopping. But they are not the only way railroads are finding to improve their operations.

Container trains, unheard of 30 years ago, are one of the hot money-makers on today's railroads. From every major port in the United States, tens of thousands of freight containers are unloaded at dockside, put on to flatbed trucks, and short-hauled to a nearby railroad container terminal. There, the standardized containers are loaded, singly or stacked on top of each other, on specially designed freight cars, many of which are semi-permanently coupled together.

From these yards, fast trains are dispatched in all directions to other parts of the country, both for use in the U.S. and as a part of a rail-bridge to other countries. Time and again, railroads have proven that it is cheaper for an Asian country to ship their European-bound goods via an American West Coast port and trans-ship them via rail to an East Coast port where they are reloaded for the trip to Europe; in effect, the railroads create a land-bridge.

For the most part, however, containers have given the railroads a greater flexibility in handling freight. Now, they don't have to buy or maintain large fleets of boxcars that must be individually loaded, then shipped elsewhere, then individually unloaded. With today's marketing approach, someone else owns the container, loads it, seals it and then the railroad merely transports it, dropping it off at the other end, where the person receiving it is in charge of unloading and maintenance.

This is not to say traditional freight cars are obsolete; on the contrary, there are many commodities that still must be shipped by boxcar, gondola, tank car, or hopper, and the railroads have learned to use these tools effectively. Today's freight cars are longer, wider, more capacious, longer-lasting and are more far more flexible than any of their predecessors.

One such concept is the unit train, a train with only one type of load and purpose. Most are grain trains, moving the product from the plains to markets both foreign and domestic. Other bulk commodities routinely carried by unit trains include wood chips, coal, and ore.

Another effective example of unit trains is in the transport of oil from field to refinery, from refinery to user, or from one country to another. Semi-permanently coupled together, this string of 60 to 90 tank cars travels back and forth between its two terminals with only that job to do, and doing so far more efficiently and cost-effectively then any other form of transportation. One traditional railroad car has, however, become obsolete—the caboose.

Ever since railroads were fledgling entities, there had been cabooses. Many diehard train fans still insist that a train is not a train unless there is a caboose on the end of it.

Primarily serving as the conductor's office, the caboose is where he did his paperwork, gave orders to the engineer, and, if working a local or branch-line job, kept track of what freight cars were going to which industries and when; and which cars he was picking up.

Cabooses were a necessity when a railroad was running through barren territory for hundreds of miles. They were a place to sleep and eat, and a warm, lighted haven when the rest of the world was dark and grim. Many branch-line operations depended on the comfort of a caboose to provide hotel space for the crew. Many operations had the crew work one direction on a line, then sleep over and return the next day.

There was little standardization of cabooses from railroad to railroad. While most had top cupolas so trainmen could see over the tops of freight cars, others, such as those of the Southern Pacific, were early converts to side bay windows, a necessity as many freight cars became taller than even the tallest cupola. Over the years they have received refrigerators, air conditioners, and electric heaters.

But faster trains meant shorter work days for crews; today, on a typical main line, a freight train crew may work anywhere from three to six hours and call it a day. Operations such as these meant there was little future for the caboose. Starting in the early 1980's, railroads, working with unions, began "caboose-off" programs, where cabooses started to disappear from a certain percentage of trains. Today, about 80 percent of American freight trains operate without a caboose.

The Future

Predicting the future of railroading is like predicting the future of anything else. Soothsayers can take a good stab at it, but that's about it.

Through stiffening air, truck, and pipeline competition, railroads have had to pull back and retrench, relying on selling their skills at providing inexpensive transportation of bulky materials. Gone are the days when local trains served every hamlet in America.

And gone with those trains are many of the railroads that were instrumental in opening up this country to pioneers. Through mergers of weaker companies with stronger ones, the names of the railroad community have shrunk to only a handful. In the East there is Conrail, a giant conglomerate that has risen from the ashes of the New York Central, Pennsylvania,

New Haven, Lehigh Valley, Erie-Lackawanna, Lehigh & Hudson River, Reading, and Ironton.

Gone too is the Baltimore & Ohio and the Chesapeake & Ohio, formed into CSX. Norfolk Southern has been created from the Norfolk & Western and the Southern. The Burlington Northern has replaced the Great Northern, Northern Pacific and the Chicago, Burlington & Quincy. It may be order out of chaos, but to many, it is efficiency over tradition.

Worse yet, gone are many once-proud railroads that, for one reason or another, just couldn't make it. The Milwaukee Road is no more, merged into the Soo Line and all but forgotten, except for faithful former employees. Other railroads that have been swallowed up by various companies in the past three decades include the Wabash; Nickel Plate; Katy; Missouri Pacific; Lackawanna; Western Pacific; Gulf; Mobile & Ohio; and the Erie. And though country-and-western star Johnny Cash may sing that "the Rock Island line is a mighty fine line," the Chicago, Rock Island & Pacific stands today as the largest railroad abandonment in American history.

But from the ashes of yesterday's failures comes a new railroading spirit. Today's railroads go after the long haul, interstate traffic that, in many cases, is uneconomical if shipped by truck.

Main line railroading today consists of several large railroad systems capable of acting and reacting to changing business climates. These are Norfolk Southern, CSX, Conrail, Union Pacific, Santa Fe, Southern Pacific, Burlington Northern; and following them is a number of strong regional railroads, including Guilford, Florida East Coast, Illinois Central, Kansas City Southern, and Soo Line.

There are also two other types of railroad operations.

One is the short line. At a maximum 300 miles (usually far less), these little railroads proudly say they are just as wide as the big boys. They survive because they transport one particular product (such as timber) or serve many industries in one small area.

A good example of a short line is the 18-mile-long Santa Maria Valley Railroad, midway between San Francisco and Los Angeles on the central California coast. The Santa Maria Valley (SMV) survives mainly because of sugar beet traffic and the fact that a large sugar beet refinery is located on-line. During sugar beet season, solid beet trains are turned over by the Southern Pacific to this little line, which keeps busy shuffling cars in and out of the refinery. And while the beets are extremely important to the SMV, they are only one source of revenue.

The railroad has gone out of its way to make sure it serves the many other industries in its growing industrial area, affording personalized service and a willingness to work around shippers' schedules.

Another type of railroad operation is one that has been spun off from a major company.

In many cases, mergers have resulted in redundant rail lines serving the same cities, some of which, although still heavy with industries, are not economically feasible for the big carrier to serve. Enter the regional carrier.

Many railroads, such as the Soo Line, Burlington Northern, Illinois Central, and Conrail, have spun off large chunks of viable but underproducing rail lines to new local groups,

which have the ability to renegotiate union contracts, be available to receive state funds, and, most importantly, keep the lines producing.

Farmers in North Dakota, for example, now have the Red River Valley & Western (RRV&W) as the railroad that serves their grain elevators. Comprised of former Burlington Northern branch lines, the new RRV&W is locally owned, state-subsidized and extremely willing to work with its farmers and silo operators to insure the grain gets out on time. By working together, the Burlington Northern and the Red River Valley & Western can now remain viable.

And it's the same in other areas of the country. The Soo Line purchased the Chicago, Milwaukee, St. Paul & Pacific—known as the Milwaukee Road—and consolidated its properties. It too had to spin off extra lines and, instead of applying for abandonment, helped state and local agencies form Lake States Transportation Division. Again, by renegotiating union contracts, taking advantage of state funding incentives, and working together, both operations now prosper.

Modern railroads have to operate efficiently or they die. This has caused many traditional railroad buildings and facilities to be sold or torn down. Ornate passenger stations such as those in St. Louis and Chicago have been made into visitor's centers, office complexes, and parking lots. Los Angeles has taken another approach, planning to convert its giant passenger station into a tourist mall. In addition, many local freight car yards are abandoned for more centrally located and larger ones. In general, a lot of the romance of railroads has gone by the wayside.

There is one area, however, that both railroad management and railroad enthusiasts agree on. Steam engines, that most demonstrable example of American industrial might, draw crowds, make friends for railroads and show the world railroading is still an industry with heart.

To that end, a number of railroads have refurbished steam engines that once languished in city parks and fairgrounds, and use them very effectively for industrial promotion, excursions, outings and as a link to the public at large.

Among the leaders is the Union Pacific, which stables the immaculate 3985, a 4-6-6-4 Challenger articulated steam locomotive, and the 844, a 4-8-4 Northern-type steamer, both of which saw passenger and freight duty during their regular working days.

The Southern Pacific has responded with the 4449, one of dozens of 4-8-4's it stabled to wheel fast passenger trains throughout its system. Sharp-eyed readers may remember its starring role in *Tough Guys*, a 1987 Burt Lancaster, Kirk Douglas movie.

Not to be outdone, Norfolk & Western (N&W) also operates a couple of steam engines. N & W, one of the predecessor companies to Norfolk Southern, was a pioneer and innovator in modern steam design, and fought dieselization to the end. Today, its 611, a streamlined bullet-nosed class J 4-8-4, and the 1218, a class A 2-6-6-4 articulated, are kept in perfect shape for promotional work. Other main-line heavies include a couple of Nickel Plate steam engines (the Nickel Plate's full name was the New York, Chicago & St. Louis, which was merged with the Norfolk & Western, which is now part of Norfolk Southern); one from the Pere Marquette (absorbed by the Chesapeake &

Ohio which is now part of CSX); Savannah & Atlanta 4-6-0 750; a former Reading 4-8-4 (Reading is now part of Conrail); a beautifully restored Frisco (St. Louis-San Francisco, now part of Burlington Northern) 4-8-2 number 1522; a gorgeous K4 Pacific that used to operate on the Pennsylvania Railroad (now part of Conrail); and a whole potpourri of others, ranging from tiny switchers to large main-line steamers.

And narrow-gauge railroading, while mostly a part of yesterday, can still be enjoyed today, although primarily as tourist lines.

In the East, there is the East Broad Top at Orisbonia, Pennsylvania. Besides offering rides, much of the original facility is still intact, allowing visitors to get a glimpse of a part of American railroading that has disappeared. In Colorado there are a number of narrow-gauge steam operations still going strong, most notably the Durango & Silverton and the Cumbres & Toltec Scenic Railroad. Both these lines use fragments of the original Denver & Rio Grande Western narrow-gauge empire.

The Durango & Silverton operates the former Silverton Branch of the Rio Grande. Headquartered in Durango, the line hugs numerous steep cliffs and penetrates deep, narrow gorges on its way to Silverton. No more graphic illustration of why building the line to narrow gauge was so necessary can be found.

A similar setting is in store for those who visit the Cumbres & Toltec Scenic Railroad. This line starts at the Rio Grande connection at Alamosa, Colorado and heads east to Chama, New Mexico, where the tourist operation has its headquarters. If the line continuing east from Chama were still in existence, it would eventually link with Durango.

Both operations use former Rio Grande 2-8-2's and have created a number of specially designed cars for passengers. Both are all-day outings.

There are other narrow-gauge train companies that include a tourist line in their operations. Hawaii—once known for hundreds of miles of sugar cane railroads—has one, as does the Roaring Camp & Big Trees in California. There are also various restoration projects in Colorado.

What has made this possible, however, is not just corporate might deciding that it wants steam locomotives. On the contrary, it has been the dedicated work of thousands of train enthusiasts who kept the interest in steam engines going when most railroad companies (fearing the public would react to steamers as antiques) wanted nothing to do with them.

Perhaps the most ironic twist to the resurgence of steam-engine consciousness among American railroads is that three steam locomotives in the United States are newer than most diesels. In 1989, orders for the construction of three steam locomotives from mainland China—one of the very last steam locomotive builders in the world—were placed by three tourist railroads in the United States. One was delivered to the Boone & Scenic Railroad in Boone, Iowa; another to the Valley Railroad in Essex, Connecticut; and the third to the Knox & Kane Railroad in Pennsylvania. All of these engines will be operational.

It has become a new world for transportation. It is a new world for railroading.

Being the Engineer on a Modern Main-line Freight Train

Most major railroads operate by timetable or schedule, and to keep a train operating on time takes a resourceful and knowledgeable locomotive crew. Not only does the engineer have to know every foot of the railroad he's going to cross, but there must be an almost intimate relationship between him and the train he controls. How long the train is, how much it weighs, when to brake, how much to brake, when to accelerate, what to look out for while operating, what temporary orders are in force indicating where work is being done, what the weather is ahead, and where other trains are in the area.

One of the most difficult stretches of railroading in the United States is the mountainous run over the Tehachapi Mountains in Southern California. Here, two railroads, the Southern Pacific and the Atchison, Topeka & Santa Fe, both run over the former's track from the small Antelope Valley town of Mojave 68 miles through the mountains to Bakersfield. (When one railroad operates over the rails of another, it's called having "trackage rights.")

It's 7:00 A.M. on a warm, California morning in Barstow, a small desert community about 60 miles from the Tehachapi Mountains. The town, whose population is 7,000, is a halfway stop for travelers driving to or from Los Angeles and Las Vegas. It is also the home of a large Santa Fe Railway yard.

Deep inside that yard, a crew bus squeals to a stop adjacent to four 3,600-horsepower diesel locomotives. Three men—the train engineer, a conductor, and a brakeman—get out and climb aboard the first unit.

The train, known as the 199, began in Chicago, Illinois the day before. Its destination is Richmond, California, just north of Oakland and across the bay from San Francisco. Santa Fe numbers its various trains so that dispatchers can easily follow where they came from and where they are going. The 1 in 199 for example, is for Chicago, the second 9 indicates Richmond, with the middle 9 designating the priority the train has over the system, 1 being the least, 9 being the most.

The 199 has been in Barstow for about 15 minutes. The crew that shepherded it from Needles, California on the Arizona border has just departed. The new crew, after receiving an "okay" from the inspectors that everything is functioning normally, will take it on Santa Fe rails west 60 miles to Mojave, then, by trackage rights, up and over the Tehachapi Mountains—a natural barrier between Southern California and the San Joaquin Valley—to Bakersfield. There, the train will switch back to Santa Fe tracks and make a quick 30-second stop to let this crew off and another one board. This relay race of passing the train from one crew to another assures a minimum of downtime and an adherence to the tight schedule.

There is no caboose on this train, as with the majority of freight trains in the United States; a blinking light firmly affixed to the rear coupler of the last car has replaced the traditional conductor's quarters. The conductor now rides with the engineer and brakeman. Notice also that there is no fireman and no second brakeman, all part of the latest agreements hammered out by both the Santa Fe and the various operating unions on the western end of their 22-state system.

With a go-ahead from the dispatcher, the engineer slowly notches out the throttle on the combined 14,400 horsepower he has at his command. Gradually, as slack is slowly taken out of the train, and with steady, constant power evenly applied so as not to create a jerk and possibly rip a coupler out of a car, the 199 train begins to move.

The first 60 miles to Mojave is comparatively easy for the crew, there being only a slight upgrade and no sharp curves. But there are seven long passing sidings (sidetracks or switches) between Barstow and Mojave, so the crew can expect to meet other trains as they traverse this desolate section of desert.

Behind us are 50 specially designed flatcars holding 100 truck trailers in a method of transportation appropriately known as "piggy-back." Among railroaders, it is simply called a pig train. Today's train is mostly United Parcel Service (UPS) vans as well as those loaded with perishables, such as lettuce and tomatoes. Truck-trailer and self-contained container traffic is the lifeblood of many American railroads. The boxcar, while still very important, is no longer the backbone of revenue.

Being a priority train, the 199 has more horsepower than it needs to maintain the schedule and takes only about half the power the four units are able to generate to keep the train at a constant 70 miles per hour.

Heading towards Mojave, an eastbound Santa Fe train is waiting in a siding at Boron. The block signals, something like traffic signals for automobiles, are all green in the 199's direction, indicating right of way. The engineer doesn't decrease his speed by even one mile per hour as he zips by the other train, but members of both engines carefully look over the other train to make sure everything is okay. When cabooses were on the back of every train, the men would wave at each other from the back platform indicating all was well. But in the 1990's, with most cabooses a tradition of the past, communication is by two-way radio.

A few miles east of Mojave, the train begins to slow down as it begins to climb into a sharp curve to link up with Southern Pacific rail. The two railroads share track from this point to just outside of Bakersfield, as the narrow passage carved out by man through the Tehachapi is just not enough for two separate lines. Every trackage agreement is individually negotiated by the two railroads, but usually the guest railroad is charged according to a formula based on how many trains are used and how heavy they are.

By the time 199 reaches Mojave and gets orders from the Southern Pacific dispatcher, its speed is down to 20 miles per hour. Moving slowly through the yard, the engineer notches the power all the way to the limit as soon as he receives radio permission to continue.

The uphill battle begins immediately. What took only a portion of the engineer's locomotives to keep from speeding through the desert will now devour everything he can get out of them to keep the train at 20 or 25 miles per hour, fighting to maintain speed uphill only to apply the brakes and keep the retard speed as we go down the other side.

This is where many years of experience come into play. It may look easy, but the engineer has 10,000 tons of dead weight behind him, kept in check mainly by his skill. It becomes a carefully orchestrated ballet of throttle and brakes,

giving the train the gun as it grinds uphill, only to fight to make the train slow down so it doesn't try and run away downhill. If the engineer jerks the throttle too hard, he may pull the train apart; if he hits the brakes too hard, he could have cars slamming into each other too quickly—and maybe derail half the train. If controlling the train wasn't hard enough, there is the weather and nature. Today's diesel engineer may not have the romance of the old steam engines with him, but his job is just as tough.

The line through the Tehachapi Mountains is a busy piece of railroading, with trains snaking through canyons, boring through tunnels, and cresting grades more than two dozen times a day, summer, winter and fall, rain, sunshine and snow, not to mention the constant threat of rock slides and earthquakes.

As the engineer winds the torque on his diesel charge tighter and tighter, he passes numerous trains in the Mojave Yard, his perishable status giving him rights over all of them. With the noise level ever increasing and the engineer watching out for people trying to beat him to the grade crossing immediately ahead, the cab becomes an intense working area. The other crew members are busy, too, for everyone knows that three sets of eyes—watching for signals, other trains, and any other trouble—are better than one.

The amazing thing, however, is while the work is quasi-outdoors, everyone is casually dressed and spotless. Things have changed since the early days of railroading; the engineer even wears a tie. When steam was king, even modern steam that lasted into the 1950's and '60's, this was a dirty, grimy job that beat the daylights out of a man's clothes.

The view out of the front of a diesel locomotive is nothing like anything a steam locomotive engineer had. Something like that of a large automobile, the diesel has an almost wrap-around windshield, making it a pleasure to watch the railroad. All diesels have ample heaters for the cold months and many have air conditioning. Seats are comfortable, if not luxurious, and only a few feet away in the nose of the locomotive are a toilet and a small refrigerator. A radio keeps the crew in constant contact with the dispatcher.

The toughest grade out of Mojave westbound is 2.2 percent, which means that in the next 18 miles to a destination appropriately named Summit—the highest point the railroad reaches in the mountains—the line will climb almost 1,300 feet. This may seem an unimpressive number until one realizes the engineer will also be dragging 10,000 tons behind him!

Quickly leaving the small town of Mojave behind, the train curves towards Cameron, one of the many unpopulated but designated spots on the line. Places like Cameron used to have a small station or telegraph operator's office back in the days before radios and signals were commonplace, where the operator gave the passing trains permission to proceed, and in turn, kept in touch with the dispatcher by telegraph. While unmarked, Cameron and dozens of other names are still kept alive as reference points on the railroad so when a dispatcher may warn an engineer about a track gang working the rails, he can simply say, "They're about half a mile east of Cameron," rather than approximate a longer distance from Mojave or another point.

Keeping a constant 20 miles per hour, the grade flattens out to 1.1 percent and, for the westbound trains, the worst of the fight is about over. But this has still been the short side of the trip. After cresting at Summit, there is still more than 40 miles of downhill to go.

Still working upgrade, the train passes Monolith and its gigantic cement plant, looming large on the landscape. Originally constructed to provide a local source of cement for construction of the Owens Valley Aqueduct (which feeds water to the Los Angeles Basin), it is now the largest single customer on the line between Mojave and Bakersfield, generating enough traffic to have its own local freight train work it every day.

Just before Summit, speed picks up, and the engineer conducts a running brake test, checking the air brakes at speed. Everything, say the air gauges, is operating just fine.

So far, the climb has been steady but not particularly impressive. Slipping downhill past Summit will be a far different story.

A Southern Pacific freight train is in a long passing siding at Summit and, even though the trains and crews work for two different railroads, each carefully inspects the other as they roll past.

The small mountain hamlet of Tehachapi comes and goes with nothing but a blaring of the air horn at grade crossings. Once an important midpoint in the mountains for the railroads, it is home now to only a small cadre of maintenance people. The station is still standing but it is closed, used only to store equipment.

Almost all the way to Bakersfield, the train now uses dynamic brakes to slow down. Dynamic brakes—crucial for mountain railroading—use the diesel's electric energy to slow down the train without using the air brakes. This not only saves wear and tear on the cars, it gives the engineer two independent sets of brakes with which to work his train.

At a place called Cable, the one track becomes two and the train takes the passing siding and holds it until an expected uphill train comes by. Even though 199 is on a hot schedule, the dispatcher knows it is easier to stop on the downgrade and wait for the uphill train rather than stop him on the grade and expect him to start again. Five minutes later, diesel engines at full throttle, the other Santa Fe train appears, the engineer giving a friendly wave. The immediate din of two trains-worth of diesel locomotives going by dies down to the clacking of cars. Within minutes the track is clear again, the last car of the other train fading off into the distance. The signal turns green and the engineer gets a go-ahead from the dispatcher. Brakes released, a slight nudge of the throttle, and the train is once again running.

Past Cable, the train enters the first of more than a dozen short tunnels that dot the line. The scenery is getting much more rugged now and a quick look out of the right side of the locomotive shows we are truly running along the side of the mountain. Take one step out of the diesel and there is no place to go but down.

Ducking in and out of the tunnels with regularity now, the noise of the diesels reverberates off the concrete-lined tunnel walls. Talking is impossible. The crew is too busy anyhow, not only watching to make sure the signals are green but looking for falling rocks. Slide detectors are everywhere here, and a rock only has to fall against one to make all the signals in the area turn red, a delay being far preferable to an accident. And in this case the weather, which can be moderately warm and sunny in Mojave, has turned dark and menacing. It's colder, and it starts to rain.

There is no straight track up here, just one curve after another. A green signal appears in the distance, but just as the train approachs, it pops red. The crew isn't sure: could it be another train coming, or is a supervisor pulling a safety check on the engineer to make sure he complies? It could also be moisture, a constant problem in the mountains, playing havoc with the signal's electrical wiring. The dispatcher is called.

"No problems here," says the dispatcher, who gives the train authority to pass the signal even though it is red. It is probably moisture; the dispatcher makes a note to tell maintenance.

The train goes only a few more miles before it is again in a passing siding. It is told to hold for an uphill train at a lonely wide spot named Marcel. The red nose and gray flanks of the diesels indicate it's a Southern Pacific train this time, unlike the 199's yellow-and-blue Santa Fe paint job.

Back up to 25 miles per hour and Tehachapi Loop is seen. Here, at one of the man-made marvels of North America, the train will loop under itself as it continues to descend the mountain. It's an strange feeling to go through a short tunnel at the base of the loop and look up and see the rear of the train! Tehachapi Loop is a natural gathering place for railroad enthusiasts.

A few twists and turns and the 199 is at Woodford. As it slowly makes its way through a passing siding, an SP train passes in the other direction. This time the meet is perfect and, although slowed to a crawl, the train never stops.

Bealville and Caliente are next. Once thriving Southern Pacific company towns in the days of steam, they are now just shells of their former selves. The train makes a series of twisting curves as it slowly works its way downhill. Down to 15 miles per hour (due to the sharpness of the curve), it is also an excellent place for the crew to look back and give a running inspection.

It's double track now, and a Santa Fe train roars eastbound. Right behind him is another Santa Fe hotshot. Coincidentally, it stops raining and the sun begins to peek out from behind a cloud.

Ever so gradually the scenery flattens out and the curves ease to straight tangents again. The southern San Joaquin Valley town of Bakersfield looms up on the horizon and for the crew, the day is almost over.

As we cross back over to Santa Fe rails, the train eases up to the station just off the center of town. Standing on the platform, grips in hand, is the replacement crew. No sooner is the train brought to a stop than they climb on, the old crew telling the new that everything is okay. Less than two minutes after passengers have disembarked, the new crew notches the diesels out, continuing the relay race north. They will take the train to Fresno, and another crew will take it on its last miles to the San Francisco Bay Area.

Exciting and fascinating, but for railroad crews, just another day's work.

The Union Pacific sent two of its preserved steam locomotive fleet for the 1981 grand opening of the California State Railroad Museum at Sacramento. Working their way east after the visit, 4-8-4 8444 and 4-6-6-4 3985 are near Donner Pass in California's Sierra Nevada mountains.

Steamtown USA in Scranton, Pennsylvania is a large and well-known steam tourist operation. Among its charges is this former Canadian Pacific 4-6-2, which does regular duty on the line. *Below:* This former Eureka & Palisades 2-6-2 plies three miles of circular track at the Silverwood Theme Park near Athol, Idaho. The steam engine was built in 1915 by H.K. Porter for the Eureka, Nevada Railway. *Opposite:* The engineer puts all of his experience to the test as Norfolk & Western 4-8-4 611 slows down and almost stalls while fighting an upgrade. *Overleaf:* In the Deep South, Norfolk & Western class J 4-8-4 611 pounds across the Suwannee River east of Valdosta, Georgia on its way back to Jacksonville, Florida with a steam excursion train.

Preceding page: The 4449—a former Southern Pacific steam passenger locomotive—took a two-day rest stop on its way to the 1984 World's Fair. The red, black, and orange locomotive has been seen in a number of movies. *This page:* Southern Pacific 4-8-4 4449 and Union Pacific 4-8-4 8444 (top) lie over at Los Angeles Union Passenger Terminal after bringing in celebration trains for the station's 50th anniversary. Former Southern Pacific 4-8-4 4449 (bottom), dressed up as the Freedom Train, hits a grade crossing just north of Bakersfield on its way home to Portland, Oregon in 1975.

Union Pacific 4-6-6-4 3985 thunders eastward up Sherman Hill on its way to Cheyenne, Wyoming. *Opposite:* It's cold and stormy just east of Laramie, Wyoming, as Union Pacific 4-6-6-4 3985 pulls an excursion train, one of many the railroad operates throughout its system. The 3985 was originally built for both freight and passenger service.

Steaming quietly inside the roundhouse at Jamestown, California, Sierra Railroad 2-8-0 28 is one of two such steam engines used at the Railtown 1897 State Historic Park. The Sierra Railroad still operates as a short line with diesel power. *Opposite:* The Sierra Railroad in northern California is a favorite of the motion picture industry, having been used for its purposes since the 1930's. One of the reasons for its appeal is the sight of this triple-header steam excursion working toward Oakdale.

Clockwise from left: A Feather River Railway Shay crosses a bridge over the south fork of the Feather River in northern California. (Such a feat cannot be repeated today—this entire line is underwater as part of the Oroville Dam project.) Notice the offset boiler on this Brimstone Railroad Shay 36, standard on Shay locomotives. Pennsylvania Railroad class K4s 4-6-2 1361 wheels through Vail, Pennsylvania.

An almost timeless photograph of big-time steam power: Strasburg Rail Road 2-10-0 90 is in charge of a rail excursion out of Leaman Place, Pennsylvania, in rural Lancaster County. The steam engine had previously worked for the Great Western Railway in Colorado.

Preceding page: The last light of day on Valley Railroad 2-8-0 97 near Essex, Connecticut. *This page:* Events such as this excursion (top) regularly draw the faithful from throughout the region. The thermometer says it's 25 degrees outside as Norfolk & Western class A 2-6-6-4 1218 (bottom) leads an Atlanta, Georgia to Chattanooga, Tennessee excursion train. Its smoke is 99 percent pure steam.

Chicago, Burlington & Quincy 4-8-4 5632 works a steam excursion near Denver, Colorado. As railroads depleted their steam fleets, many, including the CB&Q (now part of the Burlington Northern), kept a few engines on hand for just such occasions.

Chicago, Burlington & Quincy 2-8-2 4963 was in charge of a coal train in Missouri back in the 1960's. Many main-line steam locomotives worked out their last revenue miles leased to short lines. *Right:* A former Canadian National 0-6-0 switcher 7470 is considered (at 87 tons) small by steam engine standards. *Overleaf:* Restored after years of inactivity, three steam engines pose for cameras on the Nevada State Railroad Museum's Virginia & Truckee rail line south of Reno. The middle engine, number 22, is best known for its service in the 1960's television series *Wild, Wild West.*

Preceding pages, left: Operated by a museum crew, Virginia & Truckee 4-6-0 25 is waiting for a switch to be thrown on the Nevada State Railroad Museum's 18-acre historical site. *Preceding pages, right:* One feature of early steam power that was quickly dropped was the large amount of brasswork that had to be kept polished, such as that found on Virginia & Truckee 22. *This page:* Looking like something out of the Old West, Nevada Northern 4-6-0 40, a 1910 Baldwin, now operates as the Ghost Train of Old Ely, part of the Nevada Northern Railway Museum in Ely. The steam engine was restored to operating condition in 1986 after being in storage for almost 25 years.

A McCloud River Railroad 2-6-2 25 approaches the ice-encrusted water tank at Big Canyon, California, near the slopes of Mt. Shasta on January 27, 1973. *Opposite:* Sante Fe steam-switcher 5 (top) was originally built for barge service in the San Francisco Bay area in the 1890's. Found unsuitable for such work, the engine (named *Buttercup*) was later retired to Needles, California. Made up to look like a regular freight train, California Western 2-6-6-2 46 (bottom) is actually pulling an excursion train. *Overleaf:* Flying across a trestle, Mississippian 2-8-0 77 is in charge of a short freight. It has neat and well-maintained steam engines, retained for chartered excursions, such as this one, near Amory, Mississippi.

Preceding pages, left: A geared Shay locomotive on the Cass Scenic Railroad works upgrade in West Virginia. Shay locomotives were used for work on steep grades, where conventional power would slip. *Preceding pages, right:* As part of a test to determine if modern steam propulsion could be built for the oil-conscious 1980's, former Chesapeake & Ohio 4-8-4 614T hauled 60-car trains of coal between Huntington and Hinton, West Virginia. *This page:* Former Nickel Plate 2-8-4 765 was photographed at Thurmond, West Virginia in October, 1986, while it was pulling a passenger excursion train operated by the Fort Wayne Railroad Historical Society.

This ~~Preceding~~ *page:* While the Duluth, Missabe & Iron Range makes its revenue from hauling Minnesota iron ore, it could occasionally take time out to operate a steam excursion. The 2-10-2 514, traditionally a freight machine, powers one such event at Saginaw, September 2, 1962. The car between the tender and the first passenger car carries extra water. ~~This~~ *page:* An excellent example of a World War II United States Railway Administration (USRA) locomotive is former Nickel Plate 2-8-2 Mikado 587. Built by the Baldwin Locomotive Works near Philadelphia, Pennsylvania in August, 1918, the 587, which is back in steam as an excursion engine, is one of only five USRA 2-8-2's still in existence.

Preceding page: This former Canadian Pacific 4-6-2 is now owned by the Allegheny Central (AC) in Maryland. The AC operates on a portion of the old Western Maryland main line. *This page:* The Reading Railroad, now part of Conrail, once owned 30 magnificent 4-8-4's (top) for heavy-duty freight service. While four exist today, only the 2102—now owned by the Blue Mountain & Reading—is still operable. Taking it easy between tourist trains, East Broad Top 2-8-2's 12 and 17 (bottom) are resting at Orbisonia, Pennsylvania. This three- foot-gauge line was once a coal-hauling railroad.

Working upgrade, a former Reading T-1 4-8-4 delights the faithful with a smokey show during a passenger excursion in Pennsylvania. It is currently owned by the Blue Mountain & Reading Railroad.

Preceding page: Booming over a bridge at Coopers, Virginia on June 10, 1988, Norfolk & Western class A 2-6-6-4 1218 is on the second day of the four-day "Independence Limited" from Roanoke, Virginia to Chicago, Illinois. *This page:* Chesapeake & Ohio 614 (top) is in charge of a Chessie Safety Express excursion train from Pittsburgh, Pennsylvania to Rockwood. Double-heading (bottom) means two steam engines and two crews working at the same time. Here, two former Pennsylvania Railroad engines, a 4-4-0 and a 4-4-2, team up to power a steam excursion on the Strasburg Rail Road.

The Mt. Washington Cog Railway is a three-and-one-half-mile railroad that goes up the side of a mountain (hence its use of cogs to pull itself along). The downward slanting boiler becomes level when the train is working upgrade. *Opposite:* Recreating the South of the past, former Southern 2-8-0 630 operates at the Tennessee Valley Railroad Museum near Chattanooga on a stretch of track originally completed in 1858. *Overleaf:* Originally operated by the Savannah & Atlanta, 4-6-2 750 now operates as part of the state-sponsored New Georgia Railroad near Atlanta, Georgia. Neatly trimmed with white sidewalls, the engine looks right at home with a half-dozen passenger cars.

Preceding page: After an absence of 30 years, Norfolk & Western class A 1218 steam engine returns to Dublin, Virginia on an excursion. Easing through a narrow cut, the 1218 is just nearing the end of a short but tough climb out of the New River Valley. *This page:* "Were they loud!" said the photographer who took this picture of Norfolk & Western class J 4-8-4 611 and class A 2-6-6-4 1218 working uphill just west of Shawsville, Virginia.

Preceding page: Every element of what makes steam engines so captivating comes together in this photograph of Norfolk & Western class J 4-8-4 611 leaving Atlanta's Peachtree Station. *This page:* In the wee hours of August 20, 1982, a Norfolk & Western class J 4-8-4 611 is being readied for her first passenger train in a quarter of a century.

Savannah & Atlanta 4-6-2 750 is in charge of a seven-car passenger train, part of the Norfolk Southern excursion program. *Opposite:* Pennsylvania Railroad 4-4-2 7002 was displayed at the 1939 World's Fair. That particular locomotive was scrapped years ago, but another 4-4-2 (top) was renumbered to take its place. These tracks at Stevenson, Alabama (bottom) are among the oldest in the South, and those on the right were put down in 1846. (That Southern 2716 is, in reality, Chesapeake & Ohio 2716 with a new coat of paint.)

Preceding page: One of the narrow-gauge railroads that helped tame Colorado was the Colorado & Southern (C&S), now just a memory except for a few pieces of restored line. C&S 2-8-0 71 nears Central City, Colorado on the line to Black Hawk. *This page:* Moving heavy tonnage up steep grades is what these massive machines were designed for. Here, Union Pacific 4-6-6-4 3985 has just eased through Forelle, Wyoming.

Preceding page: Stepping out lively, Durango & Southern narrow-gauge 2-8-2 481 works a train through Colorado's Animas Canyon. This is one of the only two remaining segments of the original Denver & Rio Grande Western line (the Cumbres & Toltec Scenic Railroad is the other) still in operation. *This page:* Currently operated as the Cumbres & Toltec Scenic Railroad (owned jointly by Colorado and New Mexico), this special charter freight train was recreated to show what yesterday on the Denver & Rio Grande Western narrow-gauge looked like. *Overleaf:* A close-up view of former Denver & Rio Grande Western narrow-gauge 2-8-2 489. Small by main-line standard-gauge steam standards, these locomotives were among the most powerful on American narrow-gauge rails. Interestingly, many of these engines, including the 489, began life as standard-gauge engines; they were converted to narrow gauge by the railroad during a power shortage.

Preceding page: Waiting for its next assignment, Denver & Rio Grande Western 2-8-2 489 is steaming by itself, its boiler fire carefully banked. The cap on the stack is actually a spark arrestor, preventing lineside fires that can start from escaping hot cinders. *This page:* These two narrow-gauge Denver & Rio Grande Western 2-8-2's, operating out of New Mexico, run on some of the most desolate rails in the country. Snow is a major problem for this line.

Preceding pages: Two Denver & Rio Grande Western narrow-gauge 2-8-2's, 480 and 483, were teamed to run a snowplow train from Alamosa, Colorado over nearby Cumbres Pass (elevation 10,015 feet), and into Chama, New Mexico. *This page:* It takes a skilled engineer to control all the gauges and dials in the cab of a steam locomotive. (That glow at the bottom of the picture is coming from the firebox.) *Opposite:* The British Columbia Railway hugs cliff-sides for much of the way between North Vancouver and Squamish, British Columbia. At Britannia Beach, a 2-8-0 is in charge of the regular steam excursion.

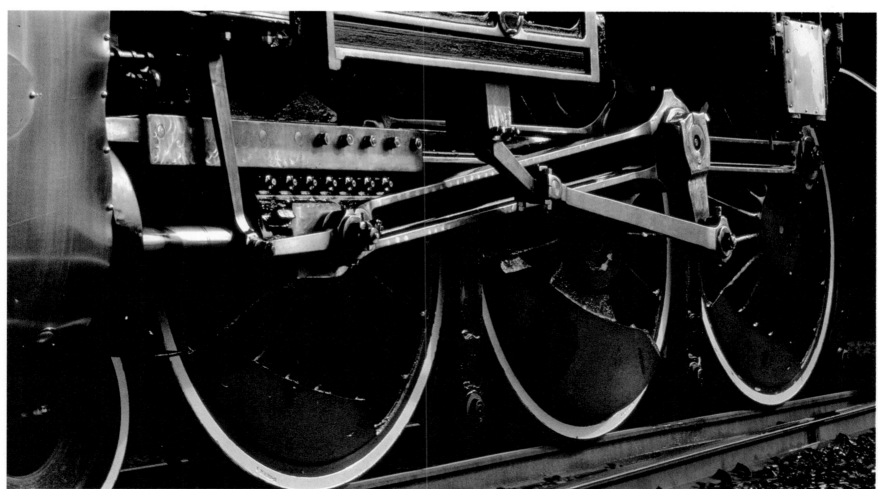

51 66 09_40 013_5

Preceding pages, left: This 2-8-0 steam engine on the British Columbia Railroad, photographed in 1986, is only a substitute; the regular engine, Royal Hudson 2860, was on a friendship tour in the United States. *Preceding pages, right:* Just beginning the first leg of the trip home, this Canadian Pacific 4-6-4 (top) is passing the Southern Pacific station at Saugus, California. All those little rods and levers by the driving wheels (bottom) get the force of the steam pressure from the cylinders just below the boiler to the drivers in an efficient and smooth manner. *This page:* The Orient Express, made famous to American audiences by the movie, *Murder on the Orient Express,* prepares to leave on an eastbound run behind a Turkish 2-10-0 Decapod. The little wings on the front of the steam engine boiler are smoke deflectors, designed to keep the exhaust away from the engineer's line of sight. *Opposite:* Close-up of the Orient Express symbol on the outside of a passenger car.

An 0-6-0T shunter on the Isle of Wight. The T stands for tank, and those rectangular boxes on the side of the boiler hold the water necessary for it to operate. *Below:* An English railroad crew prepares to begin a day's work. The English were fond of pin-striping their locomotives. *Opposite:* Trains in remote areas often find themselves in the middle of town, literally. High in the mountains of India, a daily Darjeeling Himalayan Railway passenger train is working a 55-mile line which will eventually climb more than 7,000 feet.

This Canadian-built, streamlined Indian Railways 4-6-2 is an example of postwar steam in that country. It is mostly used for passenger service, although it can also be found pulling freights. *Opposite:* A wheel arrangement not usually found in the United States, but common overseas, is the 2-10-0 Decapod. Here, a pair of Turkish engines (top) work upgrade out of Usak with the daily passenger train to Afyon. American steam designs dating back to the Allied forces invading Europe can still be found in Turkey. Doing switching at Karabuk, Turkey is a 1942 American Locomotive Company 2-8-2 Mikado (bottom).
Overleaf: Earning its keep, a National Railways of Zimbabwe 2-8-2+2-8-2 steam engine, known as a Beyer-Garratt, moves a freight on the West Nicolson branch. Beyer-Garratt locomotives are well liked because the design allows a relatively large locomotive to operate on smaller rail.

Preceding page: As an experiment in a last attempt to further steam locomotive design, South African Railways rebuilt one of their 4-8-4's (top). Known as "The Red Devil" for its unique paint scheme, it is seen here on a rail-enthusiast special from Kimberley to De Aar. While steam is slowly dying on the South African Railways, the company has maintained a small group of prestige locomotives (bottom) for special trains. From left to right at the De Aar loco shed, they include *Molly, Inge,* and *Freida. This page:* Light streams through the engine shed at Bulawayo, Zimbabwe—home for 90 steam locomotives. The unique Beyer-Garratts were once common throughout Africa.

South African Railways (SAR) class 15F 4-8-2 2928 is considered one of the most successful steam-engine designs in South Africa. At its peak, SAR rostered more than 200 of them.

An ostrich watches South African Railways 4-8-2+4-8-2 Beyer-Garratt 4122 work through Oudtshoorn on its way toward Montague Pass and the Indian Ocean. (Oudtshoorn is the ostrich farming center of South Africa.) *Below:* Powered by a less than clean steam locomotive, a South African Railways 4-8-4 powers the daily all-stops Bloemfontein to Bethlehem passenger train.

This Burlington Northern facility is located just outside of Memphis, Tennessee. *Opposite:* The Burlington Northern (BN) passes through some of the most rugged and beautiful landscape in the country. Here, train 100a is crossing Two Medicine River near East Glacier, Montana, with the Continental Divide towering behind. This is BN's principal freight route between Chicago and Seattle. *Overleaf, left:* Norfolk Southern is known for its coal movements. General Motors SD60 6580 leads a train of empty coal hoppers through Roderfield, West Virginia, back to the mines. Once loaded, they head back to power-generating plants. *Overleaf, right:* This General Motors GP30 diesel is now more than two decades old. Rated at 2,250 horsepower, the unit was once assigned to the Southern's hottest freight trains. Now it works secondary freights and is a trade-in candidate for new power.

Preceding pages, left: This Denver & Rio Grande Western (D&RGW) train 287 (top) grinds its way through the Rocky Mountains. The D&RGW serves as a "bridge" line to Eastern markets; most of its freight cars were loaded on the Southern Pacific in the San Francisco Bay area. The Richmond, Fredericksburg & Potomac Railroad (bottom) provides a North-South link from the industrial northeast to the Deep South. Doing 60-plus, RF&P train 175 wastes little time moving through Colemans Mill, Virginia. *Preceding pages, right:* There's 3,600 horsepower inside this New York, Susquehanna & Western locomotive. Built by General Motors in the mid-1960's, a locomotive like this one needs to be kept on main-line, high-speed trains for optimum performance. *This page:* The lip on the edge of a railroad wheel is called the "flange"; it keeps the wheel riding the rail. *Opposite:* These General Electric diesel locomotives symbolize the American locomotives of the 1980's and '90's. Ranging in horsepower (from 3,000 to 4,000, depending on the model), their sale price is more than $1,000,000.

Having retired its red-and-silver paint scheme with the advent of Amtrak, Santa Fe has reissued this well-known symbol of American railroading for some of its high-speed main-line locomotives. Here, 100, 101, and 102 work northbound from San Bernardino to Barstow through Cajon Pass.

Resplendent in its original red, yellow, and silver livery, General Motors F7A 347C is now a display-engine in California, but occasionally gets out on Santa Fe excursions.

Preceding page: A Santa Fe freight passes eastbound through Crozier Canyon just east of Kingman, Arizona in December, 1986. The short-lived red paint scheme was designed for the proposed merger of the Santa Fe and the Southern Pacific. When the merger fell through, both reverted to their original colors. *This page:* Museum displays don't need to be static. Santa Fe RS2 2098, an American Locomotive product that is now property of the San Diego Railway Museum in California, returns with other equipment to the museum's headquarters at Campo from a Railfair weekend in San Diego. *Overleaf:* There is only one place in the United States where a train can cross over itself: that's Tehachapi Loop, in the mountains of southern California. Still considered a true feat of engineering, the Loop sees more than two dozen trains a day.

Recalling the railroads of yesterday, freshly completed Pennsylvania Railroad General Motors E8A 5706 was shown for the first time in 1986. *Below:* Although it is wearing New York Central (NYC) colors, this General Motors E9A was never on that railroad. A former Union Pacific unit was painted in these colors when a suitable NYC unit couldn't be found for display. It is incapable of operation; even the number is fictitious.

Sometimes when locomotives are sold from one railroad to another, they are not repainted. A case in point is this former Burlington Northern SD45, now working for the New York, Susquehanna & Western line. *Below:* The New York, Ontario & Western Railroad was officially abandoned in 1957. One of the road's original units, however, was sold to the New York Central and became part of the Conrail fleet. With permission of the current owner, the New York, Susquehanna & Western, the General Motors diesel has been repainted and renumbered to resemble its original look.

Lying over for the night at Hudson Tower in Harrison, New Jersey, this Alco Century 430 design is becoming a rare breed.
The builder ceased locomotive production in the late 1960's. *Opposite:* Here, a General Motors SD38 is teamed with a "slug."
Rebuilt from an old diesel locomotive, a slug has no engine but is powered electrically from a hookup to another diesel.
The advantage is increased traction.

The Chicago, Milwaukee, St. Paul & Pacific maintained an extensive electric railroad operation throughout the Northwest on its route to the West Coast. That included yard switchers, such as this E-81 working the Butte, Montana yard.

Deep inside Conrail's massive Big Four Yard near Avon, Indiana, Conrail diesels and Union Pacific diesels on run-through trains are being serviced. Originally a New York Central facility, the yard (which is about 15 miles west of Indianapolis) is a start-of-the-art facility, capable of taking care of any locomotive or car problem.

The Railfair exhibit on San Francisco's Embarcadero in April, 1987 introduced people to both historic and contemporary railroad equipment. *Opposite:* From left to right, the trains pictured here are Southern Pacific (SP) E9A 6051, a passenger diesel; Western Pacific (WP) F7A 913, a freight hauler; and Union Pacific E8A 951, a passenger diesel. The SP and WP unit are the property of the California State Railroad Museum and the Union Pacific diesel is still in service. *Overleaf:* A few miles west of Central City, Nebraska, a pair of General Electric diesels belonging to the Union Pacific (UP) drift by. This is part of the UP's original Overland Route, where it meets the Central Pacific (now Southern Pacific) in Utah.

Deep in the Feather River country of northern California, a Union Pacific freight train works eastbound crossing Rock Creek trestle. This is the former Western Pacific (WP) main line from Oakland to Salt Lake City, before the WP was absorbed by the Union Pacific in the 1980's. *Below:* On a warm summer afternoon in June, 1987 near North Platte, Nebraska, a Union Pacific westbound hotshot makes waves across the plains. A fast crew change at North Platte and it will be on to Salt Lake City and Los Angeles.

Roaring into the last glow of sunset, a Union Pacific unit coal train drones west through Oshkosh, Nebraska.

Preceding page: High in the Blue Ridge mountains of North Carolina, CSX freight 92 pops out of the Blue Ridge tunnel on its way to Florida. Originally the Carolina, Clinchfield & Ohio, the line was started in 1886 to tap the coal industry. *This page:* Leadville, Colorado & Southern (LC&S) is one of the newest tourist short lines in the country. A former Burlington Northern branch (originally the Colorado & Southern), the line served a molybdenum plant. *Overleaf:* Working over a portion of a former Union Pacific branch line, these three fire-engine-red General Motors F7 units are owned by Mountain Diesel Transportation, a leasing corporation.

The Pennsylvania Railroad created a magnificent electric engine: the GG-1. One such example is this 4907, powering the northbound Silver Meteor through New Brunswick, New Jersey on its way to New York City. *Below:* An Amtrak passenger train flies down the New York-Washington D.C. corridor, past Portal Tower in the New Jersey Meadows.

Clockwise from left: Leaving the canyons of Manhattan behind, New Jersey Transit E60 electric 967's final destination is Bay Head, New Jersey. These are Chicago & North Western diesels on the point at Clio, California, on the Union Pacific. The Northwestern Pacific, a subsidiary of the Southern Pacific, put the northern part of its line on the California coast for sale; it was purchased by the Eureka Southern, who chose to run excursions for entertainment and to boost the freight revenue.

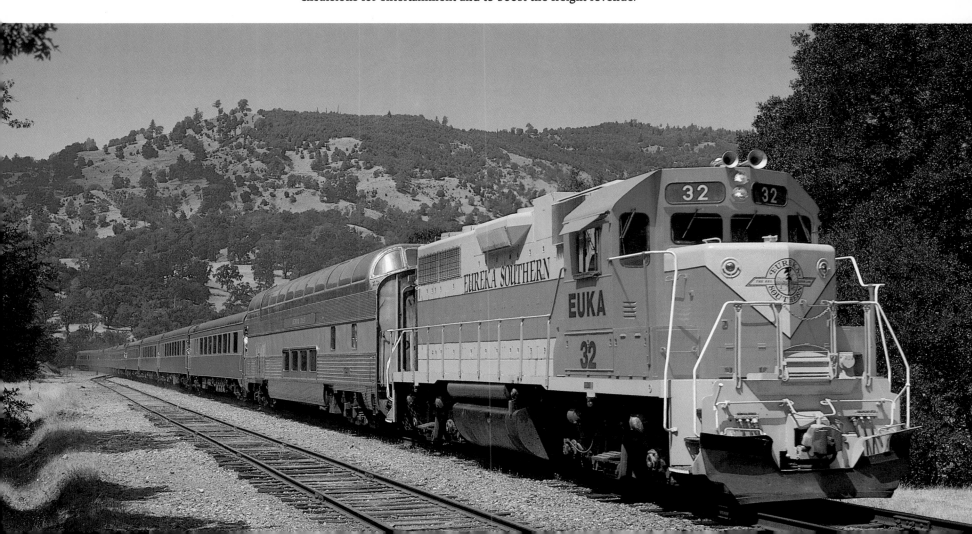

Preceding page: Originally disdained for its universal sameness, Amtrak has brought passenger-train service back from post-World War II disarray, and has, coincidentally, a rising tide of passengers. *This page:* MARC—Maryland Rail Commuter (top)—is a Washington D.C.-to-Baltimore commuter. The latest in electric locomotives, it typifies state-run rail operations. Amtrak's Silver Meteor (bottom) leaves Washington D.C. behind, bound for New York City. Power is supplied by a stubby little AEM7, one of the newer pieces of equipment on the system.

With the New York skyline in the background, a New Jersey Transit E8A unit sits out the night at Hoboken in October, 1989. Going on its third decade of service, the 2,250 horsepower E8 was one of the most popular post-World War II diesel-passenger engines.

An eastbound New Jersey Transit commuter train takes a full load of homeward-bound commuters into the sunset. *Overleaf:*
All is quiet among the Pennsylvania Railroad electric commuter cars in the wee hours of the morning. The Pennsylvania
maintains the largest electrical operation in the East.

A perfect example of unit-train technology: Farmers can get a lower transportation price by pooling together enough grain to fill an entire train load destined for one market (top). These Canadian Pacific covered hoppers (bottom) leave little doubt as to their intended purpose. *Opposite:* Looking down on the complex trackage of a busy French railroad terminal, one sees a multitude of switches, all of which can be thrown electrically from a remote tower.

The face of French electric passenger locomotives. France has been a leader in advancing the speed and comfort of intercity passenger trains, including streamlining techniques to cut down on wind resistance. *Overleaf:* No need to explain why the high-speed Japanese trains are known as "Bullet Noses." Four line up in Tokyo, waiting for the afternoon outbound run.

Index of Photography